Herbs and Spices: Nature's Remedies for Health and Wellness

by Dave Njogu

BABAZURI CREATIVE FIRM

While every precaution has been taken in the preparation of this book, the publisher assumes no responsibility for errors or omissions, or for damages resulting from the use of the information contained herein.

HERBS AND SPICES: NATURE'S REMEDIES FOR HEALTH AND WELLNESS

First edition. November 9, 2023.

ISBN: 979-8224006663

Written by Dave Njogu.

Also by Dave Njogu

101 Common Questions Answered
Mastering Business English Q&A

Standalone
The Healing Harvest: Organic Farming 101
Unlock Your Authorial Potential:The Ultimate Guide to Crafting and Selling eBooks Using ChatGPT and Draft2digit
Herbs and Spices: Nature's Remedies for Health and Wellness
Grit and Growth: Unleashing Mental Toughness for Small Business Success
Design Mastery: Principles of Page Layout and Typography for Beginners

Watch for more at https://bcreativefirm.co.ke.

Table of Contents

To those who find solace in the whispers of herbs, and joy in the dance of spices—this book is dedicated to your journey of well-being. May the wisdom within these pages infuse your life with the essence of nature's healing touch.

Introduction: Unlocking the Healing Power of Herbs and Spices

Herbs and spices have been cherished by humanity for centuries, revered for their culinary magic and esteemed for their profound contributions to our health and well-being. As we embark on this journey through the world of herbs and spices, we will uncover the profound secrets hidden within nature's pantry that have the potential to transform your life. Welcome to "Herbs and Spices: Nature's Remedies for Health and Wellness."

The Importance of Herbs and Spices in Promoting Health:

IN TODAY'S FAST-PACED and often synthetic world, it's easy to overlook the incredible healing potential that lies within the leaves, stems, seeds, and roots of these humble plants. Throughout history, our ancestors understood the intrinsic connection between nature and human health. They harnessed the therapeutic properties of herbs and spices to alleviate ailments, enhance vitality, and savor the joys of life.

The significance of herbs and spices in promoting health cannot be overstated. These botanical wonders are packed with a rich array of nutrients, antioxidants, and bioactive compounds that offer a wealth of health benefits. They can boost the immune system, reduce inflammation, aid digestion, regulate blood sugar, and even protect against chronic diseases. Herbs and spices are nature's gift to humanity, an invaluable resource waiting to be explored.

Personal Connection and Passion for the Subject

AS THE AUTHOR OF THIS book, my fascination with herbs and spices began during my time working with Mr. Kamande at Wakas Organic Demo Farm in Kenya. I served as a graphics designer and video editor under the umbrella of my own creative agency, "Babazuri Creative Firm." This innovative agency primarily operates online, and you can find us at bcreativefirm.co.ke.

In my role as a graphics designer and video editor for Babazuri Creative Firm, I was responsible for creating engaging visuals, capturing captivating photos, and editing inspiring videos that showcased the remarkable work taking place on the farm. Little did I know that this experience would mark the beginning of a profound connection with the world of herbs and spices.

While immersing myself in the activities of Wakas Organic Demo Farm, I stumbled upon a wealth of information about the health benefits of various herbs. This newfound knowledge sparked a deep and abiding interest in the extraordinary healing properties of these natural wonders. After all, who doesn't aspire to enjoy the blessings of good health?

My own commitment to a healthy lifestyle has been an ongoing journey, one that I wholeheartedly embrace despite its occasional challenges. I firmly believe in the power of wholesome nutrition and balanced living, and I am dedicated to the pursuit of these ideals. This book, "Herbs and Spices: Nature's Remedies for Health and Wellness," stands as a testament to my unwavering dedication to healthy eating and vibrant living.

My connection with herbs and spices transcends mere curiosity; it has evolved into a lifelong commitment. The knowledge I've acquired over the years, the countless hours I've spent experimenting in the kitchen, and the remarkable stories of healing I've encountered have all contributed to my unyielding passion to share this wisdom with you, the reader. Through the pages of this book, I hope to illuminate the boundless potential that herbs and spices offer for enhancing your overall well-being and the quality of your life.

Together, we will explore the captivating world of herbs and spices, uncovering their secrets and celebrating their ability to enrich our lives. It is my earnest desire that this book serves as a source of inspiration and practical guidance, encouraging all of us to embrace the transformative power of nature's pantry and make positive choices for our health and vitality.

Overview of the Book's Content:

"HERBS AND SPICES: NATURE'S Remedies for Health and Wellness" is a comprehensive guide that delves into the enchanting world of herbs and spices. We will explore their nutritional value and the medicinal properties that make them true treasures in our pursuit of health. Additionally, we will uncover their versatile culinary applications and how to incorporate them into your daily meals.

Chapters on growing and harvesting herbs at home will empower you to cultivate your own natural remedies. You will also find insights into sustainable sourcing, ethical consumption, and the future of herbal medicine. In the conclusion, we will tie together the profound impact of herbs and spices on our well-being, inspiring you to embark on your own journey toward better health.

This book is a testament to the remarkable synergy between nature and human wellness. It's an invitation to rediscover the forgotten traditions of our ancestors and to embrace the timeless wisdom of herbs and spices. Let us embark on this voyage of discovery together and unlock the transformative power of nature's pantry.

Chapter 1: The Basics of Herbs and Spices

Herbs and spices are the unsung heroes of our kitchens, elevating our culinary creations and enhancing our health in ways we might not even realize. In this first chapter, we will embark on a journey to understand the fundamental aspects of herbs and spices—their definitions, their historical and cultural significance, and the various forms in which they are used.

Definition and Differentiation:

HERBS are typically the leafy, green parts of plants used for culinary or medicinal purposes. They are known for their delicate flavors and fragrances and are usually used fresh or dried. Some common herbs include basil, rosemary, parsley, and cilantro.

Spices, on the other hand, are derived from various parts of plants such as seeds, roots, bark, and fruit. They are responsible for the bold and intense flavors that define many dishes. Familiar spices include cinnamon, cumin, ginger, and black pepper.

Understanding the difference between herbs and spices is essential as they play distinct roles in the culinary world. Herbs bring freshness and subtlety, while spices offer depth and complexity to dishes. Throughout this book, we will explore their unique properties and applications.

Historical and Cultural Significance:

THE USE OF HERBS AND spices dates back thousands of years and is deeply intertwined with the history and culture of societies around the world. They have been valued not only for their culinary attributes but also for their medicinal and preservation qualities.

In ancient Egypt, spices like cinnamon and coriander were used in the embalming process, highlighting their significance in preserving and flavoring foods. In India, spices like turmeric and cardamom have been integral to Ayurvedic medicine for centuries. Meanwhile, Mediterranean cuisines are renowned for their use of herbs like oregano, thyme, and basil.

Throughout history, the trade of spices along the Silk Road and other ancient routes was so significant that it shaped empires and inspired epic journeys. The cultural importance of herbs and spices continues to influence regional and global cuisines to this day.

Various Forms and How to Use Them:

HERBS AND SPICES COME in a variety of forms, each suited to different culinary applications. You'll encounter fresh herbs, dried herbs, ground spices, whole spices, extracts, and even essential oils derived from these botanical wonders.

- **Fresh herbs** are typically used in salads, garnishes, or added near the end of cooking to preserve their delicate flavors.

- **Dried herbs** are excellent for long-term storage and are often used in simmered dishes, soups, and stews.

- **Ground spices** are versatile and add flavor to both sweet and savory dishes.

- **Whole spices** are often toasted or ground just before use to release their full aroma and flavor.

- **Extracts** and **essential oils** are potent and should be used sparingly to impart a concentrated flavor.

In the pages that follow, we will delve deeper into the characteristics and uses of various herbs and spices. You'll discover the magic they bring to your culinary creations and learn how to incorporate them into your daily meals, whether you're a seasoned chef or a novice in the kitchen. With a solid understanding of the basics, we can now explore the rich world of herbs and spices with confidence and curiosity.

Chapter 2: Nutritional Value and Medicinal Properties

In this chapter, we venture deeper into the extraordinary world of herbs and spices, exploring their nutritional richness and the remarkable medicinal properties that have captivated humanity for centuries. As we embark on this journey, you'll discover the wealth of benefits that herbs and spices can bring to your life and well-being.

Nutritional Content: Unveiling Nature's Bounty

HERBS AND SPICES ARE much more than mere flavor enhancers. They are nutritional powerhouses, packed with a diverse array of essential vitamins, minerals, antioxidants, and other bioactive compounds that can positively impact our health.

Let's consider a the following examples:

1. Turmeric:

Active Compound: Curcumin

Health Benefits:

- **Anti-Inflammatory Powerhouse:** Curcumin is known for its potent anti-inflammatory properties, making it a valuable natural remedy for conditions involving inflammation.

- **Antioxidant Properties:** Turmeric helps combat oxidative stress and free radicals, supporting overall health and longevity.

- **Pain Relief:** Curcumin may offer relief from pain and is often used as a natural alternative to conventional pain relievers.

- **Brain Health:** Some studies suggest that curcumin may enhance cognitive function and reduce the risk of neurodegenerative diseases like Alzheimer's.

2. Cinnamon:

Active Compound: Cinnamaldehyde

Health Benefits:

- **Blood Sugar Regulation:** Cinnamon has been linked to improved insulin sensitivity and lower blood sugar levels, making it a valuable tool for managing diabetes.

- **Heart Health:** It may contribute to reducing risk factors for heart disease, including lowering LDL (bad) cholesterol and triglycerides.

- **Anti-Inflammatory Effects:** Cinnamaldehyde has anti-inflammatory properties that may help with conditions related to chronic inflammation.

- **Antioxidant Boost:** Cinnamon is rich in antioxidants, which can combat oxidative stress in the body.

3. Ginger:

Active Compounds: Gingerol, Shogaol

Health Benefits:

- **Digestive Aid:** Ginger is well-known for its ability to alleviate digestive discomfort, including nausea, indigestion, and motion sickness.

- **Anti-Inflammatory and Antioxidant:** The active compounds in ginger, especially gingerol, possess strong anti-inflammatory and antioxidant properties.

- **Pain Relief:** It may help relieve muscle pain and osteoarthritis symptoms.

- **Immune Support:** Ginger can boost the immune system and help the body ward off infections.

4. Garlic:

Active Compound: Allicin

Health Benefits:

- **Antibacterial and Antiviral:** Garlic's allicin content provides powerful antibacterial and antiviral effects, making it a natural immune booster.

- **Heart Health:** Regular consumption of garlic has been associated with a reduced risk of heart disease by lowering blood pressure and improving cholesterol levels.

- **Antioxidant Properties:** Garlic contains antioxidants that protect the body from oxidative damage.

- **Potential Cancer Protection:** Some studies suggest that garlic may reduce the risk of certain types of cancer, particularly those affecting the digestive system.

Certainly, here are 10 more herbs and spices, along with their health benefits:

5. Rosemary:

Active Compound: Rosmarinic Acid

Health Benefits:

- **Memory and Cognitive Function:** Rosemary has been linked to improved memory and cognitive function, making it a potential brain-boosting herb.

- **Anti-Inflammatory:** Rosmarinic acid in rosemary exhibits anti-inflammatory properties.

- **Digestive Health:** It may aid in digestion and alleviate indigestion and bloating.

- **Antioxidant Rich:** Rosemary is rich in antioxidants, which help combat oxidative stress.

6. Oregano:

Active Compound: Carvacrol

Health Benefits:

- **Antibacterial and Antifungal:** Oregano's carvacrol content makes it effective against harmful bacteria and fungi.

- **Digestive Aid:** It can help relieve digestive issues and improve gut health.

- **Antioxidant Properties:** Oregano is packed with antioxidants that protect against free radicals.

- **Anti-Inflammatory:** It may reduce inflammation and related symptoms.

7. **Basil:**

Active Compounds: Eugenol, Linalool

Health Benefits:

- **Stress Reduction:** Basil can help reduce stress and anxiety.

- **Anti-Inflammatory:** The active compounds have anti-inflammatory properties.

- **Digestive Aid:** Basil may soothe digestive discomfort.

- **Immune Support:** It supports the immune system with its antioxidant properties.

8. **Coriander:**

Active Compounds: Linalool, Coriandrin

Health Benefits:

- **Digestive Health:** Coriander can alleviate digestive issues and reduce bloating.

- **Anti-Inflammatory:** It exhibits anti-inflammatory properties.

- **Cholesterol Management:** Some studies suggest it may help manage cholesterol levels.

- **Antioxidant Rich:** Coriander is a good source of antioxidants.

9. **Peppermint:**

Active Compound: Menthol

Health Benefits:

- **Digestive Relief:** Peppermint can relieve indigestion, bloating, and irritable bowel syndrome (IBS) symptoms.

- **Pain Management:** It may help alleviate headaches and muscle pain.

- **Mental Clarity:** Peppermint can improve mental alertness and focus.

- **Fresh Breath:** It's commonly used for freshening breath.

10. Sage:

Active Compounds: Rosmarinic Acid, Carnosic Acid

Health Benefits:

- **Cognitive Function:** Sage has been associated with improved memory and cognitive function.

- **Anti-Inflammatory:** Rosmarinic acid in sage offers anti-inflammatory properties.

- **Antioxidant Rich:** Sage is rich in antioxidants that protect the body from oxidative stress.

- **Menopausal Symptom Relief:** Some studies suggest sage may reduce hot flashes and other menopausal symptoms.

11. Thyme:

Active Compounds: Thymol, Carvacrol

Health Benefits:

- **Antibacterial and Antifungal:** Thyme's thymol and carvacrol content make it effective against harmful microorganisms.

- **Respiratory Health:** It may help relieve respiratory issues like coughs and congestion.

- **Antioxidant Properties:** Thyme is a rich source of antioxidants.

- **Digestive Aid:** Thyme can soothe digestive discomfort.

12. Cardamom:

Active Compounds: Eucalyptol, Terpinene

Health Benefits:

- **Digestive Health:** Cardamom can alleviate digestive issues and improve overall gut health.

- **Antioxidant Properties:** It offers protection against oxidative stress.

- **Anti-Inflammatory:** The active compounds in cardamom have anti-inflammatory effects.

- **Oral Health:** Cardamom may help freshen breath and promote oral health.

THESE HERBS AND SPICES, when incorporated into your diet, not only add depth and flavor to your dishes but also contribute to your overall health and well-being. Whether you sprinkle them into your recipes or enjoy them as teas or supplements, they have the potential to enhance your quality of life in numerous ways.

These herbs and spices not only bring vibrant flavors to your culinary creations but also offer a plethora of health benefits. They serve as nature's pharmacy, enhancing the taste of your dishes while contributing to your overall well-being. Incorporating them into your diet can be a delicious and health-conscious choice.

These are just a few instances of the nutritional richness found in herbs and spices. As we delve into the profiles of popular herbs and spices in this chapter, you'll gain a deeper understanding of the nutrients they offer and how they can be harnessed for your health.

Medicinal Properties: Nature's Healing Touch

THE WORLD OF HERBS and spices is not only a realm of tantalizing flavors and aromatic wonders but also a treasure trove of medicinal properties backed by a substantial body of scientific research and studies. In recent years, there has been a resurgence of interest in the potential therapeutic benefits of these natural wonders, revealing that the healing touch of nature is not merely folklore but an essential aspect of holistic well-being.

Cumin: A Natural Antimicrobial and Anti-Inflammatory Agent

Cumin, the warm and earthy spice known for its distinctive aroma, offers more than just a delightful flavor profile. It has been the subject of scientific investigation, unveiling its remarkable antimicrobial and anti-inflammatory properties. Research has shown that cumin can inhibit the growth of harmful microorganisms, making it a valuable addition to our culinary repertoire. Furthermore, its anti-inflammatory attributes may have a positive impact on conditions linked to chronic inflammation, such as arthritis and inflammatory bowel disease.

Rosemary: Enhancing Cognitive Function and Memory

Rosemary, with its fragrant and aromatic leaves, has earned a special place in the world of herbs and spices. Beyond its culinary applications, rosemary has been linked to improved cognitive function and memory. The active compounds found in rosemary, such as rosmarinic acid, have shown potential in supporting mental clarity and memory retention. It's no wonder that rosemary has earned a reputation as the herb of remembrance.

Oregano: Nature's Defender Against Bacterial and Fungal Infections

Oregano, with its bold and robust flavor, is more than just a culinary delight. It contains compounds, including carvacrol and thymol, which have demonstrated the ability to combat bacterial and fungal infections. These powerful constituents make oregano an essential ingredient in the fight against harmful microorganisms. Whether used in savory dishes, infused oils, or herbal remedies, oregano is a natural defense against a variety of pathogens.

Basil: A Stress-Reducer with Anti-Inflammatory Benefits

Basil, with its sweet and slightly peppery flavor, has been celebrated not only for its culinary versatility but also for its potential to reduce stress and inflammation. Scientific research has unveiled basil's ability to combat stress by regulating the body's response to it. Additionally, its anti-inflammatory properties may provide relief from various conditions associated with chronic inflammation, such as arthritis and asthma.

These fascinating discoveries represent just the tip of the iceberg. The resurgence of interest in herbs and spices within the scientific community has led to ongoing research efforts aimed at unearthing the profound health benefits they offer.

Profiles of Popular Herbs and Spices: Nature's Apothecary

IN OUR EXPLORATION of herbs and spices, we're about to embark on a fascinating journey through a treasure trove of flavors, fragrances, and health benefits. These botanical wonders, each with its unique characteristics and qualities, are truly nature's apothecary, offering both culinary delight and holistic well-being.

Within the world of herbs and spices, there is a multitude of choices, and each holds its own distinct set of properties and potential health advantages. In this section, we will delve into detailed profiles of some of the most popular and versatile herbs and spices, uncovering their nutritional composition, medicinal attributes, and practical applications in both the kitchen and holistic health practices.

Basil: The Fragrant Elixir

Basil, with its sweet and slightly peppery flavor, is a beloved herb in the culinary world. But it offers more than just taste—it is also a source of vitamins and minerals, including vitamin K, iron, and calcium. Basil is renowned for its potential to reduce stress and inflammation, making it a valuable addition to your diet. We'll explore how to use basil in both classic and innovative dishes.

Cilantro: The Fresh and Zesty Herb

Cilantro, also known as coriander leaves, brings a refreshing zest to dishes with its bright, citrusy aroma. Packed with antioxidants and essential vitamins, cilantro is known for its potential to detoxify the body, reduce inflammation, and support digestive health. We'll discover how to incorporate cilantro into a variety of cuisines and explore its various health benefits.

Parsley: The Unsung Hero

Parsley, often considered a mere garnish, is a nutritional powerhouse. Rich in vitamins, particularly vitamin K, and other essential nutrients, it contributes to bone health and overall well-being. Parsley is more than just a decoration; it's a potent ingredient in its own right. We'll uncover its culinary uses and the unexpected health benefits it can offer.

Mint: The Cool and Invigorating Herb

Mint, with its cool and invigorating flavor, has an array of uses, from soothing teas to refreshing cocktails. It's also known for its potential to alleviate digestive discomfort and boost mental clarity. We'll explore how mint can be harnessed to add a touch of freshness to your culinary creations while supporting your health.

Lavender: The Fragrant Herb with Many Facets

Lavender, known for its delightful scent, extends beyond its use in aromatherapy. It can be used in cooking to infuse dishes with a unique floral flavor. Lavender is also believed to have relaxation and stress-relief properties. We'll uncover the versatile applications of lavender and the soothing benefits it can provide.

Dill: The Herb of Freshness

Dill, with its delicate and feathery fronds, adds a burst of freshness to various dishes. Rich in vitamins and minerals, dill is valued for its digestive and antimicrobial properties. We'll explore its culinary applications, from pickles to seafood, and delve into how it can promote both flavor and well-being.

These profiles are just the beginning of our journey through the rich tapestry of herbs and spices. Each of them offers unique characteristics that can enhance the taste of your dishes while contributing to your health and vitality. As we continue to explore, you'll gain insights into the versatility of herbs and spices and the myriad ways they can enrich your culinary creations and promote your well-being. Nature's apothecary awaits, ready to enhance both your kitchen and your life.

Chapter 3: Culinary and Medicinal Uses

In this chapter, we will delve into the versatile world of herbs and spices, exploring their dual role as both culinary delights and potent natural remedies. These botanical wonders have been an integral part of our culinary traditions for centuries, enriching our dishes with flavors, fragrances, and vibrant colors. However, they are not just flavor enhancers; they also have a profound impact on our health and well-being. We will uncover their culinary applications in various cuisines, discover their medicinal uses for common health issues, and even provide you with simple recipes to seamlessly incorporate them into your daily meals.

Culinary Applications in Different Cuisines: Savoring Global Flavors

HERBS AND SPICES ARE the soul of culinary traditions across the world. They bring unique character and depth to dishes, turning simple ingredients into culinary masterpieces. In this section, we will explore their roles in different cuisines, from the fiery spices of Indian curries to the fragrant herbs of Mediterranean cuisine. You'll learn how to use them to create authentic flavors and elevate your home-cooked meals to new heights.

A. Indian Cuisine: A Symphony of Spices and Flavors

Indian cuisine is a remarkable tapestry of flavors and aromas, celebrated for its exquisite use of herbs and spices. It's a cuisine that offers not just a meal but an experience—a journey through a rich and diverse culinary landscape. At the heart of this culinary artistry lie the intricate spice blends, such as garam masala and curry powder, which infuse a burst of flavors into every dish, turning even the simplest ingredients into extraordinary creations.

(i) Garam Masala: The Essence of Indian Spice Blends

Garam masala, often referred to as the "warm spice mix," is the quintessential Indian spice blend. It's a harmonious fusion of spices like cinnamon, cardamom, cloves, nutmeg, and black pepper. The blend varies across different regions of India, each adding its unique twist, but the core essence remains the same. Garam masala infuses a warm, earthy, and slightly sweet flavor into dishes. It's the final touch, the finishing flourish, that elevates both savory and sweet dishes.

In Northern India, garam masala is commonly added to rich and creamy gravies like butter chicken or chicken tikka masala. It also finds its way into biryanis, where the blend enhances the aroma and depth of the fragrant rice and tender meat.

(ii) Curry Powder: A Multifaceted Spice Blend

Curry powder, while bearing the name "curry," is not a single spice but rather a blend of various spices like coriander, cumin, turmeric, and fenugreek. The combination and proportions of these spices can vary widely, resulting in an array of curry powders. This versatile blend adds vibrancy and complexity to Indian dishes.

In Southern India, curry powder is often used in vegetarian dishes like masala dosa and vegetable curries. It provides a burst of color and a depth of flavor that's essential to the cuisine. In the West, it's integrated into popular dishes like chicken curry or lentil dal.

The art of using garam masala and curry powder is not limited to meat-based dishes. It's equally valuable in vegetarian and vegan cooking, where these spice blends enhance the flavors of legumes, vegetables, and grains, creating an enticing array of choices for those seeking plant-based options.

The impact of these spice blends is profound, transcending mere taste and aroma. They create a sensory experience that engages the palate, ignites the senses, and transports you to the vibrant streets and bustling markets of India. With garam masala and curry powder, Indian cuisine invites you to savor the depths of flavor and indulge in a culinary adventure that reflects the rich tapestry of the country's diverse culture and traditions.

B. Mediterranean Cuisine: A Culinary Odyssey of Fresh Herbs and Mediterranean Magic

Mediterranean cuisine, with its vibrant and health-conscious approach to cooking, is a celebration of fresh ingredients and the liberal use of herbs and spices. This sun-soaked region offers a delightful juxtaposition of flavors, where the bounty of the land and sea meets the aromatic embrace of herbs like oregano, thyme, and basil. The result is a cuisine that not only tantalizes the taste buds but also promotes wellness through the natural healing properties of these herbs.

(ii) Oregano: The Fragrant Emblem of Mediterranean Flavor

Oregano, a fragrant herb with a robust and slightly peppery flavor, is emblematic of Mediterranean cuisine. Its aromatic leaves, whether fresh or dried, infuse dishes with a warm and earthy essence. Oregano is a staple in the region's culinary repertoire, adding depth and character to iconic dishes like Greek salads and Italian pasta.

In Greek cuisine, oregano is liberally sprinkled over vibrant salads, bringing a touch of the Mediterranean breeze to every bite. Its essence is also captured in marinades for grilled meats, lending a delightful smokiness to the dishes. In Italian cuisine, oregano is a key player in pizza and pasta, where its aromatic notes elevate the simplicity of the ingredients to extraordinary heights.

(ii) Thyme: The Timeless Herb of Balance

Thyme, with its subtle yet distinctive flavor, is another cherished herb in Mediterranean cuisine. It is a herb that embodies the essence of balance and harmony. It finds its way into countless Mediterranean recipes, imparting an earthy, lemony, and slightly minty flavor to dishes like roasted lamb and vegetable medleys.

The delicate leaves of thyme complement the richness of Mediterranean roasted vegetables, offering a counterpoint to the caramelized sweetness of peppers, eggplants, and zucchinis. It's a herb that encourages the blending of flavors in dishes, creating a culinary mosaic of sensations that reflect the very essence of Mediterranean life.

(iii) Basil: The Herb of the Sun-Drenched South

Basil, with its sweet and slightly peppery taste, is a Mediterranean herb that exudes the warmth and essence of the sun-drenched south. It's a versatile herb that finds its place in Mediterranean cuisine in dishes like Caprese salad, pesto, and tomato-based pasta sauces.

The aromatic basil leaves bring a burst of freshness to Mediterranean recipes, harmonizing beautifully with the flavors of sun-ripened tomatoes, mozzarella cheese, and the rich, fruity notes of extra-virgin olive oil. It embodies the very spirit of Mediterranean cooking—simple yet profound, vibrant yet grounded.

Mediterranean cuisine not only celebrates the use of fresh herbs like oregano, thyme, and basil but also showcases how these herbs contribute to a healthy and balanced diet. They infuse dishes with depth, flavor, and aromatic delight, turning every meal into a sensory journey along the Mediterranean coastline. It's a cuisine that invites you to savor the pleasures of fresh, local ingredients, embrace a heart-healthy approach to cooking, and experience the magic of the Mediterranean diet.

C. Mexican Cuisine: A Fiesta of Warm Spices and Flavorful Fiesta

Mexican cuisine is a spectacular and dynamic culinary adventure that takes your taste buds on a fiesta of flavors, colors, and textures. At the heart of this vibrant cuisine are the warm spices like chili powder and cumin, which infuse the dishes with zest and zestiness. From salsas and enchiladas to tacos and tamales, Mexican cuisine is a celebration of the rich tapestry of spices that paint a vivid and fiery portrait on your palate.

(i) Chili Powder: The Fiery Heart of Mexican Flavor

Chili powder is the fiery heart of Mexican cuisine. It's a blend of ground chili peppers, often combined with other spices like cumin, oregano, and garlic. The type of chili used can vary, from the smoky depth of ancho chilies to the fiery punch of habaneros. Chili powder is the spice that adds warmth, depth, and complexity to Mexican dishes.

In salsas, it provides the kick that awakens your senses and ignites a passion for bold flavors. It's the soul of chili con carne, where the blend of chili powder and cumin transforms a humble dish into a culinary marvel. Mexican chili powder is the secret ingredient behind the smoky, spicy, and rich profile of mole sauce, one of Mexico's most iconic culinary treasures.

(ii) Cumin: The Earthy Undertone of Mexican Spice Blends

Cumin, with its earthy and nutty notes, is an essential spice in Mexican cuisine. It's the grounding force that complements the fiery elements of chili peppers. Cumin infuses dishes with a warm and slightly citrusy flavor, adding depth and balance to the cuisine's bold and spicy character.

In tacos, cumin can be found in the spice blend for seasoning meats like ground beef or shredded chicken, creating a symphony of flavors in every bite. It's the backbone of Mexican rice, where the aromatic grains absorb the essence of cumin, making it a flavorful side dish. In tamales, the blend of cumin, chili powder, and masa harina creates a sensational and comforting delicacy.

Mexican cuisine doesn't just rely on these spices for flavor; it embraces them as a way of life. The warmth and zest of chili powder and the earthy undertones of cumin create a culinary legacy that's a testament to the rich cultural tapestry of Mexico. It's a cuisine that encourages you to embrace the bold and the flavorful, to savor the zest of life and the vibrant spirit of Mexican culture.

D. Asian Cuisine: The Symphony of Flavors in a Delicate Balance

Asian cuisine is a culinary symphony celebrated for its delicate balance of flavors. It's a world of contrasts, where sweet meets savory, spicy harmonizes with mild, and umami embraces the senses. This nuanced culinary palette is achieved through the artful use of herbs and spices like ginger, garlic, and lemongrass, which are integral to Asian cooking, adding depth and complexity to dishes like stir-fries, soups, and noodle creations.

(i) Ginger: The Spice of Zing and Freshness

Ginger, with its distinct zingy flavor, is a cornerstone of Asian cuisine. It is a versatile spice that adds vibrancy and warmth to an array of dishes. In stir-fries, the addition of ginger provides a refreshing and slightly spicy kick, creating a perfect contrast to the savory and sweet elements. It's also a common ingredient in marinades, where its sharpness enhances the flavors of grilled meats and vegetables.

In Asian soups, ginger serves a dual purpose. It infuses a warm and aromatic note into the broth, while its potential to alleviate nausea and digestive discomfort makes it a comforting choice for those under the weather. Ginger's adaptability is showcased in various cuisines, from the fiery ginger-infused dishes of Sichuan cuisine to the subtle hints in Japanese broths and Thai curries.

(ii) Garlic: The Pungent Heart of Asian Cuisine

Garlic, with its pungent aroma and rich, savory taste, is another indispensable herb and spice in Asian cuisine. In stir-fries, it forms the aromatic foundation, releasing its depth of flavor as it sizzles in hot oil. Garlic's magic lies in its ability to enhance the umami notes of meats, seafood, and vegetables, making it a fundamental component in Asian wok dishes.

In Asian noodles, garlic often finds its way into the savory sauces and broths that define dishes like ramen, pho, or pad Thai. Its robust flavor infuses the dish with a heartiness that is both comforting and invigorating. The aromatic allure of garlic is also a central theme in the culinary traditions of Korea, where fermented garlic is used to create the beloved condiment known as kimchi.

(iii) Lemongrass: The Fragrant Elixir of Asian Creations

Lemongrass, with its citrusy and herbaceous flavor, is the elixir that adds a refreshing twist to Asian cuisine. It's often used in stir-fries, curries, and soups, bringing a zesty and aromatic dimension to the dishes. The fragrant lemongrass is a common ingredient in the rich and coconutty curries of Thai and Indonesian cuisines.

In Vietnamese pho, lemongrass is one of the star components in the aromatic broth that defines the dish. Its fragrance enhances the sensory experience, making each spoonful a symphony of flavors. Lemongrass is also celebrated for its potential health benefits, from reducing inflammation to aiding digestion.

Asian cuisine's delicate balance of flavors is a testament to the art of using herbs and spices like ginger, garlic, and lemongrass. They transform ordinary ingredients into extraordinary dishes, turning every meal into a sensory adventure. In Asian cooking, the harmony of tastes and aromas is celebrated, inviting you to savor the complexity of flavors and explore the rich culinary traditions of the continent.

Medicinal Uses for Common Health Issues: Nature's Healing Potentials

HERBS AND SPICES ARE not only sources of culinary pleasure but also natural remedies for various common health issues. We will explore their medicinal uses, backed by both tradition and scientific research, in addressing everyday concerns such as digestion, inflammation, and stress. Learn how to harness the healing properties of these botanical treasures to support your well-being.

A. Digestive Health: Unlocking the Magic of Herbs and Spices

Digestive health is a vital aspect of overall well-being, and nature's pantry is teeming with herbs and spices that offer a wealth of benefits for the digestive system. From soothing indigestion to reducing bloating and supporting overall digestive well-being, these botanical wonders have been relied upon for centuries to ease discomfort and promote a healthy gut.

(i) Ginger: The Champion of Digestive Comfort

Ginger, with its warm and slightly spicy flavor, is a champion of digestive comfort. It's a natural remedy that has been cherished for generations for its ability to alleviate indigestion and ease nausea. Ginger stimulates the digestive process by promoting the flow of digestive juices, which can help break down food and prevent discomfort.

Whether enjoyed in a soothing cup of ginger tea, incorporated into stir-fries, or added to baked goods, ginger is a versatile herb and spice that provides relief from the symptoms of indigestion and motion sickness. It's also commonly used as a digestive aid after indulgent meals, offering a natural and effective solution to post-feast discomfort.

(ii) Mint: The Cooling Elixir for Digestive Relief

Mint, with its refreshing and cool flavor, is another herbal hero for digestive health. Peppermint, in particular, is renowned for its ability to reduce bloating and alleviate symptoms of irritable bowel syndrome (IBS). Mint relaxes the muscles in the gastrointestinal tract, helping to soothe cramps and promote healthy digestion.

Mint's versatility in the kitchen knows no bounds. It can be used to infuse refreshing beverages, such as peppermint tea, or as a flavorful addition to salads, desserts, and savory dishes. It's an herb and spice that not only awakens the senses but also comforts the digestive system, making it a valuable ally in maintaining a happy and balanced gut.

(iii) Fennel: The Anise-Like Digestive Elixir

Fennel, with its mild and anise-like flavor, is a digestive elixir that has been cherished in culinary and herbal traditions. It's known for its carminative properties, which means it can help relieve gas and bloating by relaxing the muscles of the digestive tract. Fennel seeds are often chewed after meals in many cultures to aid digestion.

In cooking, fennel bulbs and seeds add a delightful crunch and mild sweetness to salads and roasted dishes. They can also be brewed into a soothing fennel tea, which is often recommended for digestive issues. Fennel's digestive benefits extend beyond comfort; they contribute to a balanced and happy gut.

The magic of herbs and spices like ginger, mint, and fennel lies in their capacity to enhance not only the flavor of your dishes but also your digestive well-being. They offer natural and gentle solutions to common digestive concerns, ensuring that you can savor your meals with comfort and ease. Embrace the healing properties of these botanical treasures and promote digestive health as a cornerstone of your overall wellness.

B. Inflammation Management: The Natural Wonders of Turmeric, Cinnamon, and Rosemary

Chronic inflammation, a silent yet pervasive condition, is a common underlying factor in various health concerns, including arthritis and heart disease. In the quest for effective and natural methods to manage inflammation, herbs and spices have emerged as potent allies. Among the stars of this herbal ensemble are turmeric, cinnamon, and rosemary, each with its unique anti-inflammatory properties that offer a ray of hope for those seeking relief from chronic inflammation.

(i) Turmeric: The Golden Spice of Healing

Turmeric, often referred to as the "golden spice," is celebrated for its potent anti-inflammatory properties. At the heart of this vibrant orange root lies curcumin, a natural compound renowned for its ability to reduce inflammation. Curcumin's effectiveness in alleviating inflammation is backed by a substantial body of scientific research.

In the culinary world, turmeric adds both color and depth of flavor to dishes, from Indian curries to smoothies and soups. Beyond its culinary applications, turmeric is also used as a herbal remedy for a range of inflammatory conditions, including arthritis, osteoarthritis, and rheumatoid arthritis. It offers a natural and gentle approach to inflammation management, offering hope for those seeking relief from chronic pain and discomfort.

(ii) Cinnamon: The Sweet and Spicy Anti-Inflammatory

Cinnamon, a fragrant and sweet spice, offers a unique combination of delightful flavor and anti-inflammatory properties. Cinnamaldehyde, a compound found in cinnamon, has been linked to its potential to reduce inflammation. This aromatic spice is not just a kitchen favorite; it's also a natural remedy with promising benefits.

Cinnamon finds its way into both sweet and savory dishes, from breakfast oatmeal to spiced stews and curries. Its sweet notes add a warming touch to beverages and desserts. The anti-inflammatory potential of cinnamon makes it a versatile spice that can be incorporated into the daily diet, offering a sweet and soothing solution for managing inflammation.

(iii) Rosemary: The Herb of Memory and Inflammation Management

Rosemary, with its fragrant leaves and pine-like aroma, is more than just a culinary herb; it's a natural remedy celebrated for its anti-inflammatory properties. Rosemary contains compounds like rosmarinic acid and carnosol, which have shown promise in reducing inflammation and oxidative stress.

In the kitchen, rosemary's aromatic notes enhance the flavors of roasted meats, vegetables, and hearty soups. Beyond culinary applications, rosemary can be used to make soothing teas, infusions, and aromatic oils. Its anti-inflammatory potential extends to conditions like arthritis and heart disease, offering an herbal approach to inflammation management.

The allure of herbs and spices like turmeric, cinnamon, and rosemary lies not only in their culinary charm but also in their profound impact on inflammation management. They offer a natural and gentle alternative to conventional treatments, providing hope for those seeking to alleviate chronic inflammation and regain their quality of life. Embrace the healing properties of these botanical treasures and explore the world of natural solutions for inflammation management.

C. Stress Reduction: The Calming Influence of Basil and Lavender

In a world marked by fast-paced living and ever-increasing demands, stress has become a near-constant companion for many. It's essential to find ways to alleviate stress, not only for mental and emotional well-being but also for overall health. Herbs like basil and lavender have emerged as gentle and natural allies in the quest for stress reduction, offering a soothing balm for the mind and soul.

(i) Basil: The Stress-Reducer with a Culinary Twist

Basil, with its sweet and slightly peppery flavor, is not just a culinary delight but a herb with remarkable potential for stress reduction. This aromatic herb contains compounds that can positively influence our physiological response to stress, helping to regulate the body's stress-related processes.

In the kitchen, basil's fragrant leaves are a popular addition to Italian dishes, salads, and pesto sauces. However, its uses extend far beyond the culinary realm. Basil can be harnessed to create aromatic herbal teas and infusions, which promote relaxation and alleviate mental tension. It's a versatile herb that, whether in cuisine or as a stress-reduction aid, offers a dual benefit to those seeking a reprieve from the strains of daily life.

(ii) Lavender: The Fragrant Herb with a Calming Aura

Lavender, with its delightful scent, is celebrated for its calming and stress-reducing properties. Lavender aromatherapy is a well-known technique for inducing relaxation and reducing anxiety. The scent of lavender has been shown to lower cortisol levels, which are associated with stress and the body's "fight or flight" response.

Beyond aromatherapy, lavender can be used in a variety of ways to promote relaxation. It can be incorporated into herbal teas, sachets for pillows and linens, or infused into bathwater for a soothing and stress-relieving experience. Lavender's versatility and calming aura make it an ideal choice for those seeking to unwind and find respite from the pressures of modern life.

The enchantment of herbs like basil and lavender lies not only in their culinary and aromatic appeal but also in their capacity to ease the burdens of stress. They offer a natural and gentle approach to stress reduction, promoting mental and emotional well-being. Embrace the therapeutic properties of these botanical wonders, and discover a pathway to tranquility and relaxation in a world filled with the hustle and bustle of daily existence.

Simple Recipes to Incorporate Them into Meals: Infusing Flavor and Health

IN THE QUEST FOR A healthier and more flavorful lifestyle, simple recipes that incorporate herbs and spices can be your gateway to culinary creativity and improved well-being. These recipes not only elevate the taste of your meals but also harness the unique health benefits that herbs and spices offer. From aromatic herbal teas and spice-infused oils to mouthwatering marinades and rejuvenating tonics, let these culinary creations unlock the potential of nature's bounty in your kitchen.

1. Herbal Infusion Teas: Sipping Serenity

Enjoying a cup of herbal infusion tea is a delightful way to harness the soothing properties of herbs like chamomile, peppermint, and lavender. To create a stress-relief tea, simply steep a few sprigs of fresh lavender or a teaspoon of dried chamomile flowers in hot water. This calming infusion can be enjoyed in the morning to start your day with tranquility or in the evening to unwind.

2. Spice-Infused Oils: Flavor Beyond Measure

Enhance the flavors of your dishes by crafting your own spice-infused oils. For a spicy kick, add red pepper flakes and garlic to a quality olive oil. Allow the flavors to meld for a few days, and you'll have a fragrant and versatile oil that can be drizzled over salads, pizzas, or roasted vegetables. The possibilities are endless, and you're in control of the spice level.

3. Health-Packed Marinades: Flavorful and Nutrient-Rich

Marinades are an excellent way to incorporate the health benefits of herbs and spices into your meals. Create a simple marinade by mixing crushed garlic, freshly chopped basil, and a dash of olive oil. This marinade not only infuses your proteins or vegetables with a burst of flavor but also introduces the potential anti-inflammatory and antioxidant properties of the ingredients.

4. Rejuvenating Tonics: Sipping Wellness

Rejuvenating tonics provide a refreshing and health-boosting way to consume herbs and spices. For instance, a revitalizing ginger and lemon tonic combines freshly grated ginger, lemon juice, and a drizzle of honey. This concoction not only invigorates the senses but also introduces the anti-nausea and digestion-aiding properties of ginger.

5. Flavorful Salad Dressings: Herbaceous Elegance

Elevate your salads with homemade herb-infused dressings. Mix fresh basil, parsley, or cilantro with olive oil, vinegar, and a touch of honey or Dijon mustard. Drizzle this herbaceous dressing over your greens for a burst of freshness and the potential anti-inflammatory benefits of the herbs.

> These simple recipes not only make your meals more delicious but also offer a gateway to embracing the health-boosting properties of herbs and spices. By incorporating them into your daily culinary adventures, you can savor the fusion of flavor and wellness, turning your kitchen into a place of both culinary artistry and natural healing. Let these recipes be your guide to a world where taste and health coexist in harmony.

Chapter 4: Growing and Harvesting: Nurturing Nature's Pharmacy

In this chapter, we embark on a journey into the heart of your own herbal haven, exploring the art of growing and harvesting herbs. Cultivating these green allies at home not only connects you with the essence of nature but also ensures a bountiful supply of fresh, organic herbs right at your fingertips. From the nurturing stages of planting to the gratifying moments of harvest, discover the secrets to successfully growing and harvesting your own herbal pharmacy.

Cultivating Herbs at Home: Seeds of Possibility

EMBARKING ON THE JOURNEY of cultivating herbs at home is akin to opening a treasure chest of endless possibilities. The very first step in this herbal odyssey involves the exciting task of selecting the herbs that will soon call your garden home. Each herb, with its distinct hues, fragrances, and healing properties, becomes a character in the vibrant tapestry of your personal green sanctuary.

Choosing Your Herbal Companions: The Garden's Symphony

The process begins with the careful selection of herbs that align with your culinary preferences, wellness goals, or simply resonate with your aesthetic sensibilities. Picture the vibrant green leaves of basil, with its sweet and slightly peppery notes, destined to grace your caprese salads and pasta dishes. Envision the soothing allure of lavender, a purple oasis that not only captivates the eyes but promises relaxation in every fragrant bloom. Consider the robust aroma of rosemary, a resilient herb that adds depth to your savory creations and carries the essence of the Mediterranean to your kitchen.

Germinating Seeds or Starting with Young Plants: The Birth of Green Life

Once you've chosen your herbal companions, the next chapter in this botanical adventure unfolds with the art of germination or the introduction of young plants to your garden. For those who revel in the full cycle of life, germinating seeds becomes a magical experience. Witness the humble seedling breaking through the soil, a promise of the verdant symphony that will soon unfold. Alternatively, starting with young plants provides a head start, allowing you to skip the initial stages and usher in the green inhabitants of your garden sooner.

Nurturing the Miraculous Transformation: From Tiny Seeds to Flourishing Herbs

As the days pass, watch with anticipation as the tiny seeds or young plants undergo a miraculous transformation. From delicate sprouts reaching for the sun to lush foliage unfurling in intricate patterns, each herb reveals its unique personality. It's a testament to the nurturing touch of the gardener and the symbiotic dance between nature and human hands. Witnessing this transformation is not merely a horticultural feat; it's a soul-stirring journey that deepens your connection with the cycles of life.

Enriching Your Well-being: More Than a Garden, a Sanctuary

Ultimately, cultivating herbs at home transcends the mere act of gardening. It becomes a journey of enriching your well-being on multiple levels. The herbs you tend to are not just green occupants in your garden but partners in your culinary adventures and contributors to your health. The vibrant green of basil, the soothing allure of lavender, and the robust aroma of rosemary are not just elements of nature; they are allies on your quest for a harmonious and holistic lifestyle.

Embark on this botanical odyssey with a sense of wonder, knowing that each herb you cultivate holds the promise of flavor, fragrance, and well-being. From the tiny seeds of possibility sprouts a garden that not only graces your dishes but also becomes a sanctuary where nature and nurture converge in a beautiful symphony of green life..

Tips on Soil, Sunlight, and Watering: Crafting the Ideal Habitat

CRAFTING THE IDEAL Habitat: Nurturing Nature's Divas

Creating the ideal environment for your herbs is a harmonious dance between the gardener and the green denizens of your garden. It involves not just the act of planting but a nuanced understanding of the unique needs and preferences of each herb. Delve into the intricate details of soil composition, sunlight requirements, and watering techniques, and unveil the secrets to tailoring your garden into a thriving and flourishing haven for your herbal companions.

Understanding Soil Composition: The Foundation of Growth

Soil is not merely the ground beneath your herbs; it's the very foundation of their growth and vitality. Different herbs have distinct preferences when it comes to soil composition. For the resilient rosemary, well-draining soil that mimics its native Mediterranean environment is key. This prevents waterlogging, ensuring the roots remain healthy and vibrant. Lavender, with its penchant for a slightly alkaline soil, thrives in well-drained, sandy loam that replicates the sun-kissed hillsides it hails from.

Sunlight Requirements: Catering to Solar Tastes

Just as we have preferences for sunlight or shade, herbs too have distinct requirements. Basil, the sun worshipper of the herb world, revels in full sunlight. Choose a spot in your garden where this aromatic herb can bask in the sun's warmth for the majority of the day. On the other hand, mint, with its love for cooler conditions, appreciates a dappled sunlight setting. Understanding these solar tastes is crucial in placing your herbs in locations that cater to their specific needs, ensuring they photosynthesize to their heart's content.

Mastering Watering Techniques: A Quenching Symphony

Water, the elixir of life, plays a pivotal role in the well-being of your herbal companions. However, not all herbs appreciate the same watering routine. Rosemary, accustomed to the arid climates of the Mediterranean, thrives in soil that dries out between watering sessions. Basil, with its more demanding hydration needs, prefers consistently moist soil. This delicate balance between quenching the thirst of your herbs and preventing waterlogged roots is an art that distinguishes a thriving garden from a struggling one.

Tailoring Your Garden: A Symphony of Individuality

As you delve into the intricacies of soil, sunlight, and watering, you are essentially tailoring your garden to the diverse personalities of each herb. Think of it as a botanical couture, where each herb is a diva with unique tastes and preferences. It's not just about cultivating; it's about curating an environment where every herb can express its full potential. From the aromatic embrace of basil to the stoic elegance of rosemary, your garden becomes a canvas where nature's diverse personalities harmonize.

Ensuring a Thriving Herbal Haven: A Gardener's Triumph

In mastering the art of crafting the ideal habitat, you ensure that your herbal haven is not just a garden but a thriving sanctuary. It's a testament to your dedication as a gardener, understanding and meeting the specific needs of each herb. Witness the flourishing leaves, the aromatic bouquets, and the vibrant colors as your garden becomes a living testament to the symbiotic relationship between the gardener and nature. It's not just gardening; it's the art of co-creating with the botanical world, ensuring a harmonious haven where herbs thrive and flourish.

Harvesting and Storing Herbs: A Bounty of Aromas

HARVESTING THE FRUITS of Your Labor: A Culmination of Green Mastery

As your herbs gracefully reach the pinnacle of their growth, the time for harvest emerges, signifying the culmination of your meticulous nurturing journey. This phase is not merely a routine chore; it's a celebration of the green mastery you've cultivated in your herbal sanctuary. Unveil the secrets of the perfect harvest, a symphony of senses that involves selecting the right time of day and employing precise techniques to preserve the potency and vitality of each herb.

Choosing the Right Moment: Timing is Everything

The art of harvesting extends beyond the simple act of plucking leaves; it's a dance with nature's rhythms. Selecting the right time of day is a crucial element in this orchestration. Early morning, when the sun is gentle and dew still caresses the leaves, or late afternoon, when the heat has subsided, are ideal moments. During these times, the essential oils in the herbs are at their peak, ensuring a harvest brimming with flavor and medicinal properties.

Precise Harvesting Techniques: A Gentle Touch

As you embark on the harvest, cultivate a gentle touch that honors the life force within each leaf and stem. Use clean, sharp scissors or pruning shears to snip herbs just above a leaf node, encouraging healthy growth for future harvests. Approach the task with mindfulness, expressing gratitude for the abundance your herbal garden provides. This act of mindful harvesting not only preserves the integrity of the herbs but also deepens your connection with the natural world.

Exploring Preservation Techniques: Harnessing Nature's Bounty Year-Round

The harvest marks not just the end of a cycle but the beginning of a new phase – preservation. Explore the art of drying, freezing, and preserving your herbal treasures, ensuring a year-round supply of nature's pharmacy. Drying herbs, whether by hanging bundles or using a dehydrator, concentrates their flavors and allows you to store them for culinary and medicinal use. Freezing herbs in oil or water preserves their freshness and can be a convenient way to infuse your dishes with herbal goodness. Creating herbal-infused oils, vinegars, or even herbal butters adds a gourmet touch to your culinary endeavors, ensuring that the essence of your garden is woven into every dish.

A Testament to Nature's Magic: From Garden to Table

Embark on this chapter as your guide to the art of cultivating, nurturing, and reaping the rewards of your own herbal sanctuary. Whether your garden sprawls across vast acres or finds a cozy spot on a modest balcony, the journey of growing and harvesting herbs is a fulfilling endeavor that connects you with the cycles of nature. Your herbal garden becomes more than a patch of green; it transforms into a testament to the magic of cultivating nature's pharmacy at your doorstep.

Let the green symphony begin, echoing the seasons and rhythms of the earth. May your herbs grace your table with health and flavor, reminding you of the interconnected dance between the gardener and nature. As you savor the fruits of your labor, may each leaf and petal be a reminder of the sustainable source of well-being and culinary delight that resides just outside your door.

Chapter 5: Sustainability and Ethical Sourcing: Nurturing Nature, Nourishing Conscience

In this pivotal chapter, we delve into the profound impact of our choices as stewards of the Earth. Sustainability and ethical sourcing are not mere buzzwords but guiding principles that shape the future of our herbal practices. Join the journey of understanding the importance of responsible sourcing and embracing the ethical consumption of herbs and spices, creating a harmonious relationship between nature's bounty and the conscientious consumer.

The Importance of Responsible Sourcing: Tending to Nature's Balance

IN THE INTRICATE DANCE between humans and nature, the concept of responsible sourcing emerges as a guiding light, illuminating the path toward a harmonious coexistence with the ecosystems that gift us the rich tapestry of herbs and spices. At its core, responsible sourcing is a profound acknowledgment that our every action, every choice, creates ripples that resonate through the delicate balance of nature.

Nurturing the Foundations of Herbal Sanctuaries: A Sacred Commitment

As stewards of the Earth, responsible sourcing becomes a sacred commitment to nurturing the foundations of our herbal sanctuaries. These sanctuaries are not merely patches of land; they are ecosystems teeming with life, from the smallest microorganisms in the soil to the towering trees that provide shade and shelter. Our herbal harvests should not be a detriment to this intricate web of life but rather a harmonious collaboration that ensures the sustained vitality of the Earth.

From the microcosm of soil health to the macrocosm of biodiversity conservation, responsible sourcing entails a comprehensive understanding of the ecosystems that nurture our herbs. It prompts us to question the methods used in cultivation: Are the herbs grown with sustainable and regenerative practices that enrich the soil rather than deplete it? Is the cultivation process respectful of the diverse life forms that call the herbal sanctuary home? These questions guide us in navigating the complex terrain of responsible sourcing, leading us toward choices that honor and preserve the sanctity of nature's balance.

Eco-Friendly Practices: Sowing Seeds of Sustainability

Consider the implications of choosing herbs cultivated with eco-friendly practices. This transcends a mere transactional exchange; it becomes a symbiotic relationship with the Earth. Eco-friendly practices involve approaches that minimize environmental impact, prioritizing the longevity and resilience of ecosystems. It's about adopting agricultural methods that work in harmony with nature, fostering soil health, reducing water usage, and mitigating the use of harmful chemicals.

As conscious consumers, our choices act as seeds sown into the fertile soil of sustainability. By opting for herbs cultivated with eco-friendly practices, we contribute to the regeneration of the Earth rather than its exploitation. This is not just a transaction; it's a partnership with the natural world, a commitment to tread lightly on the Earth and leave it thriving for generations to come.

A Sustainable Relationship: Guided by Earth's Rhythms

In the journey of responsible sourcing, we become attuned to the rhythms of the Earth. Our choices are guided by a profound understanding that the herbs and spices we cherish are part of a larger, intricate system. By making choices that resonate with the Earth's rhythms, we forge a sustainable relationship that extends beyond our immediate needs.

Whether it's the vibrant green of basil or the aromatic allure of cinnamon, each herb becomes a testament to our commitment to responsible sourcing. It embodies a conscious choice, a pledge to nurture rather than exploit, and a recognition that the delicate balance of nature is a heritage we must preserve. In the heart of responsible sourcing, we find a path that leads us back to the sacred interconnectedness of all life—a journey that transcends the transactional and embraces the transformative.

Ethical Consumption of Herbs and Spices: A Compassionate Approach

IN THE INTRICATE TALE of herbs and spices, the journey from garden to table unfolds as a narrative that intertwines with the lives of those who labor to bring nature's treasures to our kitchens. Ethical consumption becomes not just a choice but a narrative of compassion that extends beyond the leaves and seeds to embrace the individuals and communities intricately woven into the herbal supply chain. It is a commitment that reaches far beyond the confines of environmental considerations, extending a compassionate hand to the human element, empowering communities, and fostering social responsibility.

Humanizing the Herbal Journey: Beyond Leaves and Seeds

The story of herbs and spices is not confined to the verdant landscapes and aromatic fields. It's a narrative of human hands tending to the soil, cultivating the plants, and harvesting the bounty. Ethical consumption urges us to humanize this herbal journey, recognizing that behind every basil leaf or cinnamon stick lies the toil, dedication, and aspirations of individuals whose lives are intricately connected to the herbs we cherish.

Fair Labor Practices: Cultivating Dignity

At the heart of ethical consumption lies a commitment to fair labor practices, ensuring that the hands that nurture and harvest herbs are treated with dignity and respect. This goes beyond a mere transaction; it's a recognition that the herbal journey is a collaborative effort, where every individual deserves fair compensation for their contributions. From the farmers to the harvesters, ethical consumption seeks to create a cycle of empowerment that uplifts communities and cultivates a sense of pride in their invaluable role.

Empowering Local Farmers: Sowing Seeds of Sustainability

Choosing ethically sourced herbs and spices is an affirmation of the significance of local farmers in the global tapestry. It is a pledge to support and empower those who till the land, preserving traditional farming practices and fostering sustainability. By opting for herbs cultivated by local farmers, we become advocates for the resilience of local economies, encouraging self-sufficiency and contributing to the preservation of cultural heritage embedded in agricultural traditions.

Fostering Social Responsibility: A Global Community of Equity

Ethical consumption transforms our choices into powerful acts of solidarity, shaping a global community founded on principles of equity and justice. It is an acknowledgment that our interconnectedness extends far beyond geographical boundaries and cultural differences. By choosing ethically sourced herbs and spices, we actively participate in a movement that transcends mere consumption, fostering a global ecosystem where the well-being of every individual in the supply chain is valued and prioritized.

The Transformative Power of Choice: Crafting a Compassionate Narrative

In the conscious act of choosing ethically sourced herbs and spices, we wield the transformative power of choice. It's a narrative of compassion, weaving a tapestry that honors both the Earth and the hands that cultivate its gifts. As conscious consumers, our choices become a catalyst for change, shaping a future where the herbal journey is a tale of empowerment, dignity, and shared responsibility. In the realm of ethical consumption, we craft a compassionate narrative that extends far beyond our tables, echoing the principles of equity and justice in every leaf, seed, and story.

Harmony Between Nature and Conscience: A Holistic Approach

IN THE INTRICATE DANCE between humanity and the botanical realm, sustainability and ethical sourcing emerge as guiding principles that beckon us toward a profound and holistic relationship with herbs and spices. This is more than a mere culinary or wellness choice; it's an acknowledgment of the interconnectedness of all living beings and the environments that sustain us. As guardians of nature's pharmacy, we hold the transformative power to positively influence the world through our conscientious choices.

A Symphony of Interconnected Lives: Recognizing Oneness

At its essence, the holistic approach of sustainability and ethical sourcing is a celebration of oneness. It's an understanding that every herb, every spice, every human, and every ecosystem is part of a grand symphony where each note, no matter how delicate, contributes to the harmonious composition of life. As stewards of nature's pharmacy, our choices become the melody that resonates through this symphony, echoing a commitment to honor and preserve the delicate balance of existence.

Guardians of Nature's Pharmacy: Power in Conscious Choices

In the realm of nature's pharmacy, we don't merely consume; we co-create. Sustainability and ethical sourcing empower us to be conscientious guardians, recognizing the intrinsic power we hold in shaping the destiny of the herbal traditions we cherish. By choosing to tread lightly on the Earth, we become architects of a world where nature and conscience coexist in harmony, fostering an environment where herbs and spices flourish, and communities thrive.

Beyond Gardens and Kitchens: A Journey of Impact

As we embark on this chapter, the journey we undertake transcends the boundaries of our individual gardens and kitchens. It's a pilgrimage that expands our awareness, allowing us to witness the profound impact our choices have on the vast tapestry of the planet and the lives of those who cultivate the herbs we hold dear. We are not solitary consumers; we are interconnected custodians of a legacy that extends beyond generations.

Embracing Responsible Sourcing: Paving the Path Forward

The exploration of responsible sourcing and ethical consumption becomes a roadmap for paving a path toward a future where the herbal traditions we cherish today can be passed on to generations with resilience and abundance. It is a commitment to preserve not only the diversity of herbs but also the rich cultural tapestry woven by the hands of farmers and harvesters across the globe. Through our conscious choices, we become torchbearers of sustainability, casting a light on a path that ensures the continuity of herbal wisdom.

Nature and Conscience in Harmonious Coexistence: An Advocacy for the Future

As advocates for a harmonious coexistence between nature and conscience, we step into the role of custodians and ambassadors. Our choices resonate beyond our immediate circles, influencing communities, industries, and the very fabric of the planet. By embracing responsible sourcing and ethical consumption, we contribute to the shaping of a future where the herbal traditions we hold dear are not only preserved but flourish, creating a legacy of sustainability, equity, and respect for all life forms.

In the embrace of this holistic approach, our herbal journey transforms into a narrative of interconnectedness—a narrative that extends beyond gardens and kitchens, beyond individual choices, and into a collective symphony where nature and conscience dance in eternal harmony.

Chapter 6: The Future of Herbal Medicine: Navigating Uncharted Terrain

In this chapter, we set sail into the uncharted seas of the future, exploring the evolving landscape of herbal medicine. As the world embraces a holistic approach to well-being, we delve into the emerging trends, developments, and ongoing research that shape the future of herbal medicine. This journey is a testament to the resilience and adaptability of age-old traditions, seamlessly integrating with modern science to unlock new potentials in the healing power of herbs.

Emerging Trends in Herbal Medicine: Bridging Tradition and Modernity

THE EVOLUTION OF HERBAL medicine into the future is a captivating tapestry woven with the threads of tradition and the vibrant hues of modern innovation. This dynamic synergy represents a harmonious dance where ancient wisdom gracefully meets cutting-edge advancements, giving rise to a renaissance in herbal medicine that transcends historical boundaries.

A Return to Nature: Rediscovering Herbal Roots

In the unfolding future, societies are experiencing a rekindling of their connection with nature. This resurgence manifests as a return to the roots of herbal medicine, where the age-old wisdom of traditional practices takes center stage. The once-forgotten remedies tucked away in ancient manuscripts and passed down through generations are now emerging as potent elixirs for contemporary health challenges. This return to nature marks a paradigm shift, as individuals seek alternatives that resonate with the rhythms of the earth.

Herbal Renaissance in Mainstream Healthcare: Breaking Conventional Barriers

Herbal medicine, once relegated to the fringes of healthcare, is now breaking through conventional barriers and finding its place in mainstream medical practices. The future witnesses the integration of herbal remedies into the fabric of contemporary healthcare, challenging the dichotomy between traditional and modern approaches. From herbal supplements that complement conventional treatments to innovative botanical formulations, herbs are becoming integral components of holistic health strategies, offering a personalized and patient-centric approach to healing.

Botanical Formulations: Where Science and Tradition Converge

The future unfolds a fascinating landscape where botanical formulations stand as a testament to the convergence of science and tradition. Herbalists and scientists collaborate to create formulations that harness the synergies between different herbs, unlocking their combined therapeutic potential. These formulations, carefully curated and backed by scientific research, represent a bridge between traditional knowledge and modern validation. As a result, herbal medicine is no longer confined to mystique but stands firmly rooted in evidence-based practices.

Holistic and Personalized Healthcare: The Herbal Approach

The integration of herbs into contemporary medicine is reshaping the healthcare landscape, offering a holistic and personalized approach to well-being. The future patient is not merely a recipient of treatment but an active participant in their healing journey. Herbal medicine recognizes the individuality of each person, acknowledging that health is a multifaceted tapestry influenced by genetics, lifestyle, and environmental factors. This personalized approach aims not just to treat symptoms but to address the underlying imbalances, fostering a state of true wellness.

As we witness the emergence of these trends, the future of herbal medicine becomes a vibrant canvas where tradition and modernity coalesce. It invites individuals to explore the richness of herbal remedies, celebrating the wisdom of the past while embracing the innovations of the future. This synergy is not just a fleeting trend; it's a transformative movement that signifies a profound shift in how we perceive and embrace the healing power of nature in our quest for well-being.

Developments in Herbal Medicine: Beyond the Conventional

IN THE UNFOLDING NARRATIVE of herbal medicine, developments reach far beyond the familiar realms, delving into uncharted territories with a spirit of exploration and innovation. The conventional boundaries that once confined herbal applications are expanding, ushering in a new era where the precision and intricacies of modern science harmonize with the richness of nature's pharmacy.

Herbal-Based Pharmaceuticals: Bridging Nature and Precision

One of the groundbreaking developments propelling herbal medicine into the future is the emergence of herbal-based pharmaceuticals. This evolution marks a departure from traditional herbal applications, as scientists and researchers explore ways to harness the therapeutic potential of herbs in standardized, pharmaceutical forms. These formulations undergo rigorous testing to ensure potency, safety, and consistency, opening doors to a new era where herbal remedies seamlessly integrate into the precision-driven landscape of modern medicine.

Extraction of Active Compounds: Unlocking Nature's Treasures

At the forefront of herbal medicine's evolution is the meticulous extraction of active compounds from medicinal plants. Scientific advancements in extraction technologies allow researchers to isolate and understand the specific constituents responsible for the therapeutic effects of herbs. This precision-driven approach unravels the intricate molecular dance within plants, unlocking nature's treasures in the form of potent bioactive compounds. From alkaloids to flavonoids, each compound becomes a key to unraveling the therapeutic potential embedded in the plant kingdom.

Precision Medicine: Tailoring Therapies to Individuals

The synergy between herbal medicine and precision medicine represents a revolutionary development. This approach involves tailoring therapies to the unique genetic, environmental, and lifestyle factors of individuals. By isolating and understanding the active compounds in herbs, researchers can design targeted therapies that address specific health concerns with precision and efficacy. This personalized approach not only enhances the therapeutic outcomes but also minimizes potential side effects, ushering in a new era where herbal medicine becomes an integral part of precision healthcare.

Scientific Advancements: Isolating the Essence of Herbs

The evolution of herbal medicine is intricately tied to scientific advancements that enable us to isolate and comprehend the essence of herbs at a molecular level. Cutting-edge techniques, such as chromatography and spectroscopy, empower researchers to dissect the complex chemical profiles of medicinal plants. This scientific lens provides a deeper understanding of the synergistic interactions between various compounds within herbs, unraveling the mysteries that have intrigued herbalists for centuries.

Paving the Way for Targeted Therapies: Harnessing Nature with Precision

As developments in herbal medicine extend beyond the conventional, the path toward targeted therapies becomes clearer. The extraction of active compounds and the integration of herbal-based pharmaceuticals pave the way for a future where herbal remedies are prescribed with precision, addressing specific health challenges in a controlled and calculated manner. This shift represents not only a transformation in herbal applications but also a testament to the harmonious collaboration between nature and scientific innovation.

In this era of exploration, developments in herbal medicine reach beyond what was once deemed conventional, embracing the potential for a future where the precision of modern science harmonizes seamlessly with the healing richness of the natural world. As the chapters of herbal medicine continue to unfold, each development becomes a milestone in a journey that propels this ancient wisdom into the forefront of contemporary healthcare, offering new dimensions of healing and well-being.

Ongoing Research: Unveiling Nature's Secrets

THE LABORATORIES OF today stand as modern alchemical chambers, where scientists embark on a captivating journey into the heart of nature's pharmacopeia. Ongoing research endeavors, conducted in laboratories around the world, are dedicated to unraveling the intricate secrets held within herbs and spices. This dynamic exploration delves into the molecular foundations of herbal compounds, unveiling their hidden complexities and unlocking the potential applications that lie within.

Molecular Foundations: Decoding Nature's Language

At the core of ongoing research in herbal medicine is the quest to decode the intricate language of nature at the molecular level. Scientists, armed with cutting-edge technologies, dissect the chemical compositions of herbs and spices. Chromatography, mass spectrometry, and other advanced techniques become the tools of the modern herbalist, enabling the identification and isolation of individual compounds that contribute to the therapeutic properties of plants. This molecular journey unveils the intricate symphony of bioactive molecules that form the essence of each herb.

Mechanisms of Action: Understanding Nature's Healing Dance

Ongoing research endeavors seek to unravel the graceful dance between herbal compounds and the human body. Scientists meticulously investigate the mechanisms of action that underlie the therapeutic effects of herbs. From anti-inflammatory responses to antioxidant activities, the molecular interactions unfold a narrative of nature's healing prowess. This understanding becomes a cornerstone for designing targeted therapies, ensuring that the benefits of herbal medicine are harnessed with precision and efficacy.

Identification of Novel Bioactive Compounds: Nature's Hidden Gems

The exploration into nature's pharmacopeia extends to the identification of novel bioactive compounds. Scientists are on a perpetual quest to discover the hidden gems within herbs and spices—compounds that hold the potential for groundbreaking therapeutic applications. These discoveries not only contribute to expanding the repertoire of herbal remedies but also inspire new avenues of exploration, offering glimpses into the vast reservoir of healing potential that nature provides.

Exploration of Synergies: Unraveling Nature's Collaborative Wisdom

One of the captivating facets of ongoing research is the exploration of synergies between different herbs. Scientists investigate how the combination of multiple herbal compounds can create a synergistic effect, enhancing therapeutic outcomes. This collaborative wisdom of nature is a testament to the intricate balance and harmony embedded in herbal formulations. Understanding these synergies opens the door to the development of herbal combinations that optimize health benefits while minimizing potential side effects.

A Captivating Journey: Unmasking Nature's Complexity

The ongoing research in herbal medicine is, at its essence, a captivating journey into the heart of nature's complexity. It is an expedition that transcends the boundaries of conventional wisdom, inviting scientists to peer into the microcosm of herbal compounds and unravel their mysteries. Each discovery becomes a stepping stone, leading us deeper into the labyrinth of nature's pharmacopeia, where every compound, every interaction, and every synergy holds the potential to transform our understanding of healing.

As researchers unveil nature's secrets in the ongoing exploration of herbal medicine, the laboratory becomes a sacred space where science and nature converge. This collaborative effort not only enriches our understanding of the healing potential within herbs but also lays the foundation for a future where the treasures of nature are harnessed with precision and reverence, unlocking new dimensions of well-being and vitality.

Potential Breakthroughs: The Horizon of Possibilities

GAZING INTO THE VAST horizon of possibilities, the realm of potential breakthroughs in herbal medicine unfolds as a tapestry of excitement and curiosity. The future promises a myriad of applications that extend far beyond the known boundaries, unveiling new therapeutic vistas and innovative approaches that have the potential to redefine the landscape of healthcare.

New Therapeutic Uses: Rediscovering Herbal Efficacy

One of the tantalizing prospects on the horizon is the discovery of novel therapeutic uses for familiar herbs. Ongoing research and exploration may reveal hidden facets of herbal efficacy, unlocking their potential in addressing health challenges that were previously uncharted. The familiar herbs that have adorned kitchens and herbal cabinets for centuries may hold untapped capabilities, waiting to be harnessed for a diverse range of health conditions.

Innovative Delivery Systems: Transforming How We Benefit

The future of herbal medicine is not just about the herbs themselves but also about how we deliver their healing essence to the body. Potential breakthroughs include innovative delivery systems that enhance the bioavailability and efficacy of herbal compounds. From advanced extraction techniques to nanotechnology-based formulations, these delivery systems aim to transform how we experience the benefits of herbs, ensuring that their therapeutic potential is maximized for optimal health outcomes.

Biotechnological Approaches: Harnessing Nature's Biopharmaceuticals

At the forefront of potential breakthroughs are biotechnological approaches that harness the power of nature's biopharmaceuticals. Plant-based vaccines represent a revolutionary avenue, where the inherent immunomodulatory properties of certain herbs may be employed to develop vaccines against various diseases. Additionally, the prospect of genetically modified herbs opens up novel pathways to enhance their therapeutic potential, creating a new era of herbal medicine that seamlessly integrates with biotechnology.

Genetically Modified Herbs: Tailoring Nature's Offerings

The genetic modification of herbs represents a frontier where the very essence of nature's offerings can be tailored to meet specific health challenges. Scientists may explore the potential to enhance the production of beneficial compounds within herbs or introduce genetic modifications that optimize their therapeutic properties. This groundbreaking approach holds the promise of creating herbs that are not only resilient but also tailored to address specific health concerns with precision.

Diverse Health Challenges: Expanding the Healing Spectrum

The horizon of possibilities in herbal medicine extends to a diverse array of health challenges. From chronic conditions to emerging diseases, potential breakthroughs may provide herbal solutions that contribute to holistic and integrative healthcare. The adaptability and versatility of herbs position them as valuable allies in addressing the multifaceted nature of health challenges, offering a natural and sustainable approach to well-being.

As we stand at the threshold of these potential breakthroughs, the horizon of possibilities beckons us to envision a future where herbal medicine transcends its historical boundaries. It invites us to embrace a dynamic and evolving landscape where the healing power of nature, coupled with innovative approaches, becomes an integral part of the healthcare narrative. In this realm of endless potential, the herbal journey transforms into a continuous exploration, where each breakthrough becomes a milestone, shaping a future where the treasures of nature contribute to the well-being of individuals and communities worldwide.

The Symbiosis of Tradition and Innovation: A Harmonious Future

IN THE EVOLVING NARRATIVE of herbal medicine, the future unveils itself as a tapestry woven with the threads of tradition and the vibrant hues of innovation. It is a harmonious symbiosis where the ancestral wisdom ingrained in herbal traditions dances in seamless unity with the transformative power of scientific exploration. As we stand on the brink of this harmonious future, it beckons us to be pioneers, guiding the way through uncharted terrain where every discovery and breakthrough contributes to a holistic well-being that integrates seamlessly into modern healthcare practices worldwide.

Honoring Ancestral Wisdom: Roots of Herbal Traditions

At the heart of this symbiotic future lies a profound respect for ancestral wisdom. Herbal traditions, cultivated over generations, become the guiding stars that illuminate the path forward. The timeless knowledge passed down through herbalists, healers, and cultural practices forms the foundation upon which the future of herbal medicine stands. It is an acknowledgment that the wisdom of the past is not a relic but a living, breathing force that enriches the present and propels us into the future.

Embracing Transformative Innovation: Science as a Catalyst

The symbiosis between tradition and innovation unfolds as a dynamic interplay between the ancient and the cutting-edge. Science becomes the catalyst for transformation, allowing us to peer deeper into the mysteries of herbal medicine. Advanced technologies, rigorous research methodologies, and the exploration of molecular landscapes unravel the intricate mechanisms that underlie the therapeutic properties of herbs. This transformative innovation is not a departure from tradition but a harmonious evolution that amplifies the healing potential within nature's pharmacy.

Pioneering the Uncharted Terrain: A Call to Exploration

As we navigate the uncharted terrain of herbal medicine, the call to exploration becomes a rallying cry. Each step forward is an invitation to pioneer new horizons, embracing the unknown with a spirit of curiosity and reverence. The uncharted terrain symbolizes the endless possibilities and undiscovered treasures that await discovery. It is an acknowledgment that the future of herbal medicine is not a predetermined destination but an ongoing journey, where each exploration contributes to a broader understanding of the intricate dance between plants and human well-being.

Contributions to Modern Healthcare: Integrating Holistic Well-being

The symbiotic future of herbal medicine envisions a seamless integration into modern healthcare practices. It is a future where herbal wisdom stands alongside conventional approaches, offering a holistic framework that addresses the physical, mental, and emotional aspects of well-being. The contributions of herbal medicine to modern healthcare extend beyond symptomatic relief; they encompass a paradigm shift towards preventive and integrative approaches that prioritize overall wellness.

Transcending Historical Boundaries: A Respected Facet of Healthcare

In this harmonious future, herbal medicine transcends its historical boundaries, shedding the labels of alternative or traditional to become a respected facet of healthcare. The holistic principles ingrained in herbal traditions find resonance in mainstream practices, fostering a culture where the integration of herbal remedies is not only accepted but celebrated. It is a future where healthcare is a collaborative journey, drawing from the strengths of both tradition and innovation to provide comprehensive and individualized care.

As we embark on this transformative journey, the symbiosis of tradition and innovation emerges not as a dichotomy but as a harmonious dance. It is an invitation to witness the unfolding chapters of herbal medicine, where each discovery, breakthrough, and integration contributes to a future where the healing potential of herbs is fully realized. In this harmonious tapestry, herbal medicine becomes a beacon, guiding us towards a future where holistic well-being is not just a goal but an integral part of the global healthcare narrative.

Conclusion: A Culmination of Herbal Wisdom

As we reach the final chapter of our herbal odyssey, let's take a moment to recap the key points that have woven together the rich tapestry of herbal knowledge. Throughout this journey, we've explored the vibrant world of herbs and spices, uncovering their historical significance, nutritional prowess, and the myriad ways they contribute to our health and wellness.

Recap of Key Points: Nourishing Body and Soul

FROM THE BASICS OF herbs and spices, delving into their definitions, historical and cultural significance, to understanding their nutritional content and medicinal properties, each chapter has been a stepping stone in unraveling the profound mysteries of nature's pharmacy. We've explored the diverse profiles of popular herbs and spices, discovering not just their flavors but the intricate dance of compounds that make them invaluable allies in our quest for well-being.

In the chapter on medicinal properties, we dove into the scientific evidence supporting the therapeutic benefits of herbs and spices, uncovering their potential to heal and nourish. From cumin's antimicrobial effects to rosemary's impact on cognitive function, each revelation reinforced the notion that the healing touch of nature is not just folklore but a scientifically validated reality.

The culinary and medicinal uses of herbs and spices took us on a global journey, exploring their integration into diverse cuisines and their role in addressing common health issues. From the aromatic spices of Indian cuisine to the fragrant herbs of Mediterranean dishes, we witnessed how these botanical wonders not only tantalize our taste buds but also serve as powerful allies in promoting digestive health, managing inflammation, and reducing stress.

In the chapter on growing and harvesting, we became cultivators, tending to the seeds of possibility and learning the art of creating an ideal environment for herbs to thrive. The green symphony of our herbal gardens became a testament to our connection with nature and the sustainability of our herbal sanctuary.

The exploration of sustainability and ethical sourcing highlighted the importance of responsible choices in our herbal journey. It reminded us that our actions echo through the delicate ecosystems that provide us with the gifts of herbs and spices, emphasizing the need for ethical consumption that extends a compassionate hand to those involved in the herbal supply chain.

Our journey into the future of herbal medicine embraced emerging trends, ongoing research, and potential breakthroughs. From the integration of herbs into mainstream healthcare to the exploration of biotechnological approaches, the future of herbal medicine beckons as a harmonious synthesis of tradition and innovation.

Encouragement for Exploration and Experimentation: Your Herbal Journey

AS WE CONCLUDE THIS exploration of herbal wisdom, I encourage you, dear reader, to embark on your own herbal journey. The pages of this book serve as a guide, but the true magic happens when you step into the world of herbs and spices, exploring and experimenting with their flavors and healing properties.

Create your herbal sanctuary, whether it's a vast garden or a small balcony. Cultivate the herbs that resonate with you, understanding their unique needs and witnessing the miracle of their growth. Experiment with recipes that infuse these botanical treasures into your daily meals, creating a symphony of flavors that not only tantalizes your taste buds but also nourishes your body and soul.

Lasting Impact on Health and Wellness: Nature's Enduring Gift

THE LASTING IMPACT of herbs and spices on health and wellness is not just a fleeting moment but a continuous journey. It's the daily ritual of sipping herbal teas that calm the mind and soothe the body. It's the culinary creations that burst with flavors and carry the essence of nature's pharmacy. It's the connection forged with the Earth as we cultivate, harvest, and honor the gifts bestowed upon us.

As you continue your herbal journey, may the wisdom gained from these pages be a companion, guiding you towards a life where herbs and spices become not just ingredients but allies in your pursuit of vibrant health and holistic well-being. The enduring gift of nature's pharmacy is yours to explore, cherish, and integrate into the tapestry of your life.

In closing, remember that the world of herbs and spices is a vast and ever-unfolding landscape. Your journey is unique, and each discovery, each experiment, contributes to the collective wisdom of herbal enthusiasts worldwide. As you navigate the realms of tradition and innovation, may the healing touch of herbs be a constant companion on your path to wellness.

Wishing you a flavorful, aromatic, and vibrant herbal journey ahead.

Resources and References

NURTURING YOUR HERBAL Knowledge

As you continue your exploration of herbs and spices, diving deeper into the enriching world of herbal wisdom, here is a curated list of recommended resources for further reading. These sources will serve as valuable companions on your ongoing journey of discovery and understanding. Additionally, to ensure the credibility of the information shared throughout this book, here are the sources and references that support the claims made within each chapter:

Recommended Resources for Further Reading:

1. **Books:**

- "The Complete Book of Herbs: A Practical Guide to Growing and Using Herbs" by Lesley Bremness

- "Healing Spices: How to Use 50 Everyday and Exotic Spices to Boost Health and Beat Disease" by Bharat B. Aggarwal

2. **Websites and Online Platforms:**

- [The Herb Society of America](https://www.herbsociety.org/)

- [World Health Organization (WHO) - Herbal Medicine](https://www.who.int/medicines/areas/traditional/en/)

3. **Scientific Journals:**

- Journal of Medicinal Plants Research

- Phytotherapy Research

4. **Online Courses:**

- [Coursera - Medicinal Herbs and Spices](https://www.coursera.org/learn/medicinal-herbs-and-spices)

5. **Podcasts:**

- "The Herbal Highway" - A podcast on herbalism, holistic health, and sustainable living.

Sources and References:

1. Chapter 2: **The Basics of Herbs and Spices**

- Grieve, M. (1971). "A Modern Herbal: The Medicinal, Culinary, Cosmetic and Economic Properties, Cultivation and Folk-Lore of Herbs, Grasses, Fungi, Shrubs, & Trees with Their Modern Scientific Uses." (Dover Publications).

2. Chapter 4: **Growing and Harvesting**

- Bremness, L. (1994). "The Complete Book of Herbs: A Practical Guide to Growing and Using Herbs." (Penguin Books).

3. Chapter 6: **The Future of Herbal Medicine**

- Aggarwal, B. B. (2011). "Healing Spices: How to Use 50 Everyday and Exotic Spices to Boost Health and Beat Disease." (Sterling).

4. **Scientific Research:**

- Kaefer, C. M., & Milner, J. A. (2008). "The role of herbs and spices in cancer prevention." Journal of Nutritional Biochemistry, 19(6), 347-361.

- Ríos, J. L. (2010). "Effects of triterpenes on the immune system." Journal of Ethnopharmacology, 128(1), 1-14.

These resources and references provide a diverse range of perspectives, from practical guides to scholarly research, ensuring a well-rounded understanding of herbs and spices. Happy reading and continued exploration on your herbal journey!

Appendix:

Enhancing Your Herbal Toolkit

In this appendix, you'll find additional tools to enrich your herbal journey. Whether you're seeking clarification on terminology, navigating through the content using the index, or looking for reliable sources to acquire herbs and spices, these resources aim to support and enhance your exploration.

Glossary of Terms:

- **Bioavailability:** The proportion of a nutrient that enters the bloodstream when introduced into the body and is made available for use or storage.

- **Culinary Herbs:** Herbs primarily used for flavoring food, such as basil, thyme, and rosemary.

- **Ethical Sourcing:** The practice of obtaining herbs and spices in a manner that considers environmental impact, fair labor practices, and community well-being.

- **Medicinal Herbs:** Herbs valued for their therapeutic properties and potential health benefits.

- **Phytochemicals:** Naturally occurring compounds in plants responsible for various health benefits.

- **Synergy:** The interaction of two or more elements to produce a combined effect greater than the sum of their separate effects.

Index:

- **Basil:** Culinary and medicinal uses
- **Cinnamon:** Blood sugar regulation
- **Ethical Sourcing:** Importance of

- **Garam Masala:** Indian cuisine spice blend
- **Herbal Medicine:** Future trends
- **Inflammation Management:** Turmeric and cinnamon
- **Mediterranean Cuisine:** Use of oregano, thyme, and basil
- **Rosemary:** Cognitive function improvement
- **Sustainability:** Responsible sourcing
- **Turmeric:** Anti-inflammatory and antioxidant properties

LIST OF RECOMMENDED Suppliers for Herbs and Spices:
1. **Mountain Rose Herbs:** [mountainroseherbs.com](https://www.mountainroseherbs.com/)
2. **Starwest Botanicals:** [starwest-botanicals.com](https://www.starwest-botanicals.com/)
3. **Frontier Co-op:** [frontiercoop.com](https://www.frontiercoop.com/)
4. **Greenspoon:** https://greenspoon.co.ke
5. **Carrefour:** https://www.carrefour.ke
6. **Bestbuy:** https://bestbuyltd.com
7. **Vegan Kenya:** https://vegankenya.com
or visit your local supermarket or groccery.

Author's Note:

Author's Note: A Personal Connection to Herbs and Spices
As the author of this herbal journey, I wanted to share a glimpse into the personal experiences and insights that fueled the creation of this book. My fascination with herbs and spices didn't start in a laboratory or a bustling market but on the vibrant fields of Wakas Organic Demo Farm in Kenya. Working as a graphics designer and video editor under my own creative agency, Babazuri Creative Firm, I found myself immersed in the world of Mr. Kamande's farm activities.

Through the lens of my camera and the canvas of graphic design, I discovered the health benefits woven into the tapestry of various herbs. The pungent aroma of garlic, the golden hue of turmeric, and the warmth of cinnamon became more than just ingredients; they became threads connecting me to a deeper understanding of well-being. Inspired by my commitment to a healthy lifestyle, this book emerged as a way to share the wisdom I've gained on this herbal odyssey.

My hope is that the pages of this book resonate with your own journey, sparking curiosity and a renewed appreciation for the treasures nature offers. As you explore the world of herbs and spices, may you find not only flavors to enrich your meals but also allies in your quest for holistic well-being.

Contact Information:
I invite you to share your thoughts, questions, or personal experiences related to this book. Your feedback is valuable, and I'm eager to engage in discussions sparked by the content. Feel free to reach out via email at davenjogu@bcreativefirm.co.e for any inquiries or reflections.

Thank you for joining me on this herbal odyssey. May your journey be as enriching and transformative as the world of herbs and spices itself.

Warm regards,

Dave Njogu

Author, Herbal Wisdom: A Journey into the World of Herbs and Natural Spices

Don't miss out!

Visit the website below and you can sign up to receive emails whenever Dave Njogu publishes a new book. There's no charge and no obligation.

https://books2read.com/r/B-A-IGXZ-GBMQC

Did you love *Herbs and Spices: Nature's Remedies for Health and Wellness*? Then you should read *The Healing Harvest: Organic Farming 101*[1] by Dave Njogu!

THE HEALING HARVEST: ORGANIC FARMING 101

In "The Healing Harvest," embark on a journey that merges the timeless wisdom of organic farming with the cutting-edge concept of food as medicine. This comprehensive guide delves deep into the realm of sustainable agriculture, exploring its potential to provide not only nourishment but also profound healing.

---

1. https://books2read.com/u/mdqGWE

2. https://books2read.com/u/mdqGWE

Discover the intricate relationship between soil health, plant vitality, and human well-being. Delve into the world of organic farming, where the careful cultivation of crops goes beyond traditional agriculture. Learn how conscientious land preparation, nutrient-rich organic fertilizers, and targeted bio-pesticides form the cornerstone of a holistic approach that nurtures both the Earth and its inhabitants.

Unearth the secrets of organic Hass avocado farming, herb cultivation, and the vibrant realm of indigenous vegetables. Understand the unique requirements of each crop and how these resonate with the principles of food medicine. Whether it's the nutrient-packed leaves of indigenous greens or the nourishing richness of avocados, every facet of organic cultivation contributes to a symphony of flavors and wellness.

However, "The Healing Harvest" doesn't merely stop at the field. Dive into the marketing and certification aspects of organic produce, exploring how these facets bolster the credibility and accessibility of food medicine. Delve into stories of successful organic farmers who have transformed their passion into a thriving vocation, paving the way for a more sustainable and health-conscious future.

Written with precision by Dave Njogu, a dedicated advocate for sustainable living, this book bridges the gap between agricultural knowledge and health-consciousness. Packed with insights and practical tips, "The Healing Harvest" is a compass guiding you toward cultivating your own well-being while treading lightly on the Earth. Whether you're an aspiring farmer, a health enthusiast, or simply curious about the profound potential of organic cultivation, this book is your essential companion on the journey to harnessing the power of food as medicine through organic farming.

Read more at https://bcreativefirm.co.ke.

Also by Dave Njogu

101 Common Questions Answered
Mastering Business English Q&A

Standalone
The Healing Harvest: Organic Farming 101
Unlock Your Authorial Potential: The Ultimate Guide to Crafting and
Selling eBooks Using ChatGPT and Draft2digit
Herbs and Spices: Nature's Remedies for Health and Wellness
Grit and Growth: Unleashing Mental Toughness for Small Business
Success
Design Mastery: Principles of Page Layout and Typography for
Beginners

Watch for more at https://bcreativefirm.co.ke.

About the Author

I'm Dave Njogu, the founder and Creative Director of Babazuri Creative Firm (www.bcreativefirm.co.ke).

Additionally, I'm a budding Blogger, Author, and YouTuber.
Read more at https://bcreativefirm.co.ke.

About the Publisher

Babazuri Creative Firm originates from Kenya and operates as a Creative Agency primarily catering to small businesses.

Our expertise encompasses graphic design, the development of practical websites, video production, and more.

Additionally, we actively champion Linux and open-source software.